This book belongs to:
_____

Zoe's Magical Mind

By: Zoe Frank & Jennifer Frank

A mind that sees the world differently is a mind full of magic.

© 2025 Zoe Frank & Jennifer Frank All rights reserved. No part of this book may be reproduced, distributed, or transmitted in any form or by any means, including photocopying, recording, or other electronic or mechanical methods, without the prior written permission of the author, except in the case of brief quotations in reviews and certain other non-commercial uses as permitted by copyright law. For permissions or inquiries, contact: Zoesmagicalmind@gmail.com
ISBN: 979-8-218-62475-0 First Edition

Zoe is a bright and curious girl with golden hair, sparkling blue eyes, and a heart full of big dreams. Every day she skipped home from school with her backpack bouncing behind her, excited to share stories with her mom and dad about her day. But today felt different. Something was on her mind.

When Zoe got home, she walked in and sat at the table, and sighed. "Mom, how come all my friends can read and write so easily, but I can't?" Zoe asked, in a sad little voice.

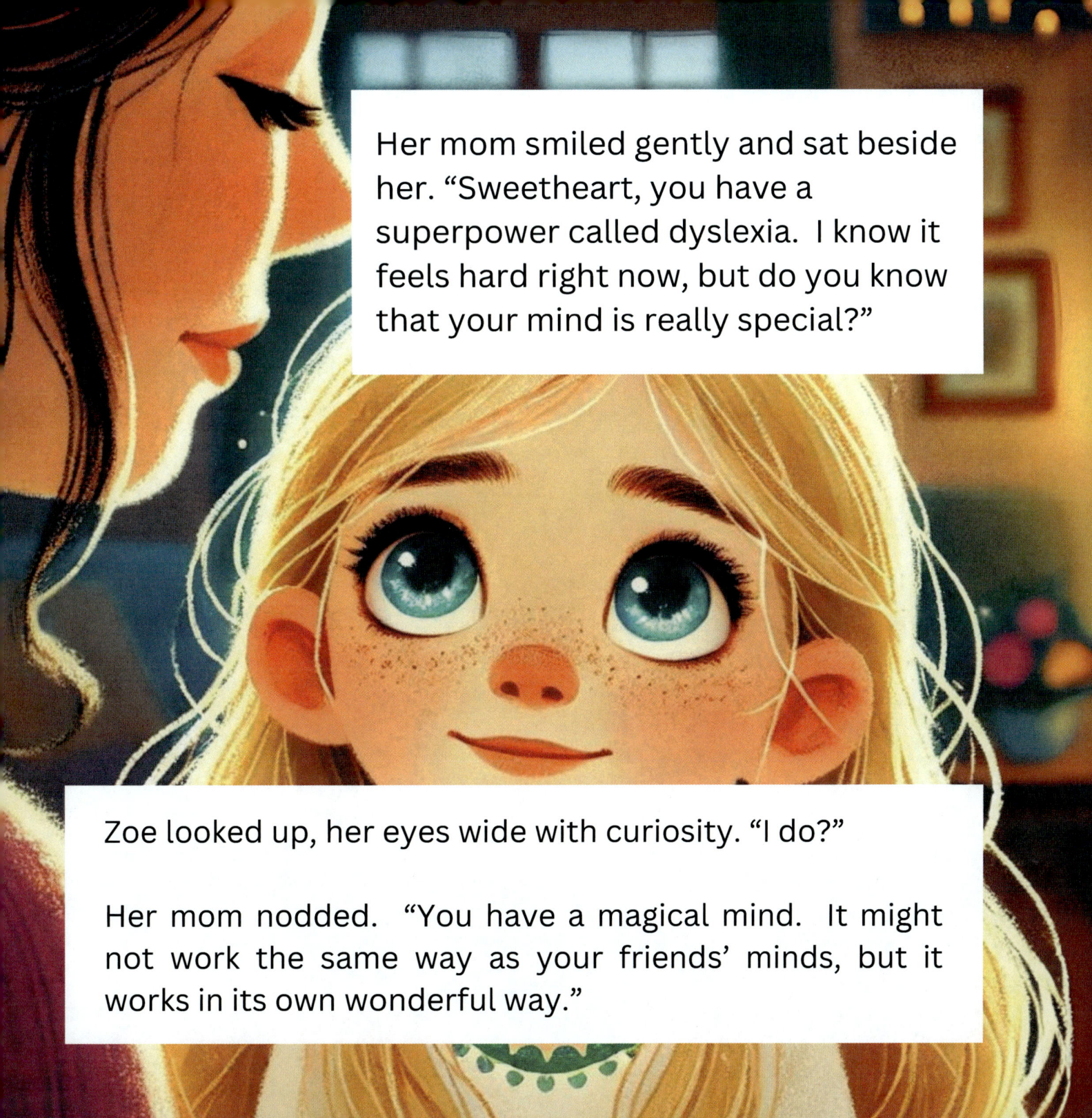

Her mom smiled gently and sat beside her. "Sweetheart, you have a superpower called dyslexia. I know it feels hard right now, but do you know that your mind is really special?"

Zoe looked up, her eyes wide with curiosity. "I do?"

Her mom nodded. "You have a magical mind. It might not work the same way as your friends' minds, but it works in its own wonderful way."

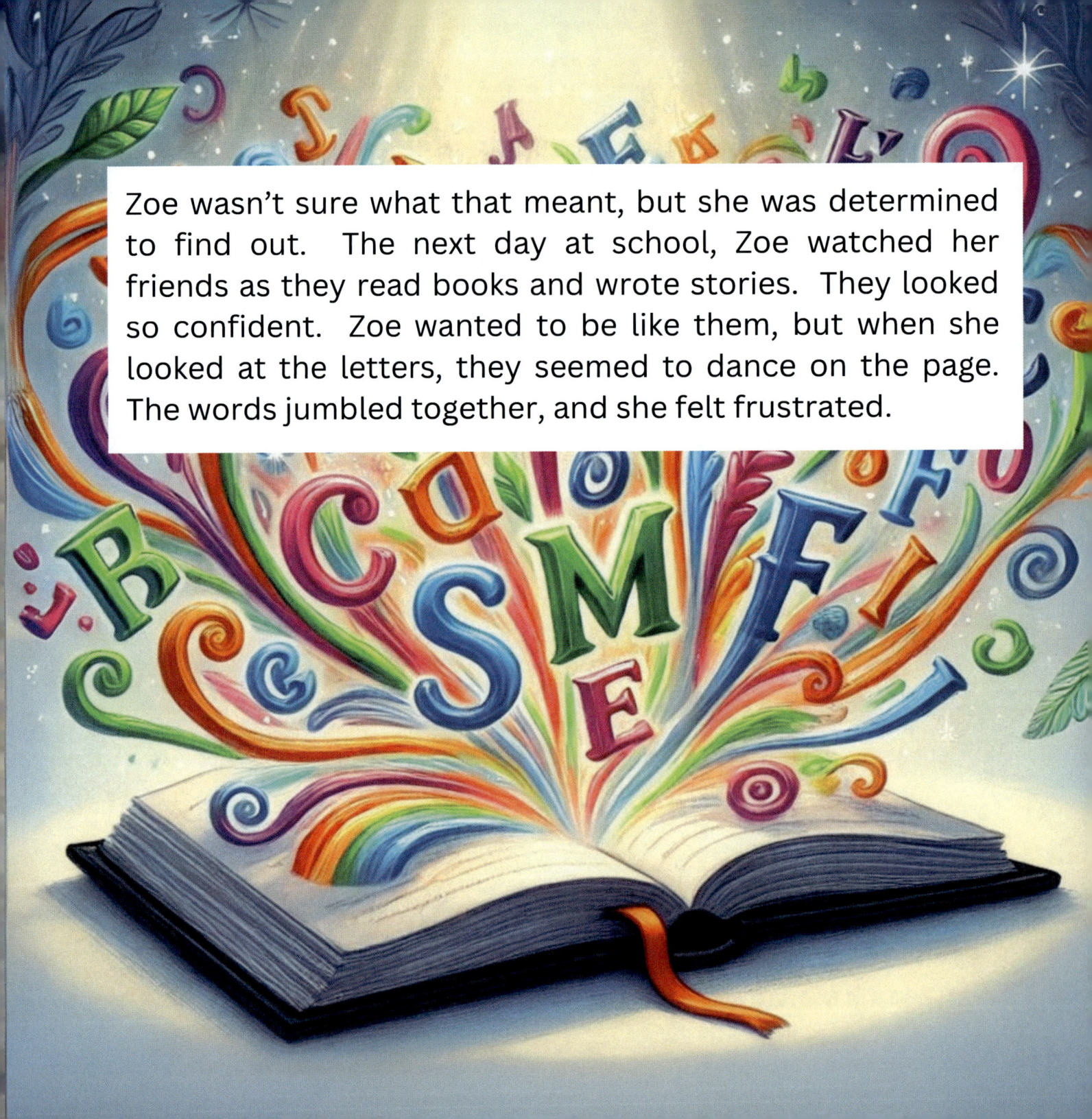

Zoe wasn't sure what that meant, but she was determined to find out. The next day at school, Zoe watched her friends as they read books and wrote stories. They looked so confident. Zoe wanted to be like them, but when she looked at the letters, they seemed to dance on the page. The words jumbled together, and she felt frustrated.

At recess, Zoe sat under a tree, feeling alone. Just then, her friend Hattie came over. "Hey Zoe, what's wrong?" she asked.

Zoe sighed. "I just don't understand why reading and writing is so hard for me. I wish I could be as good as you."

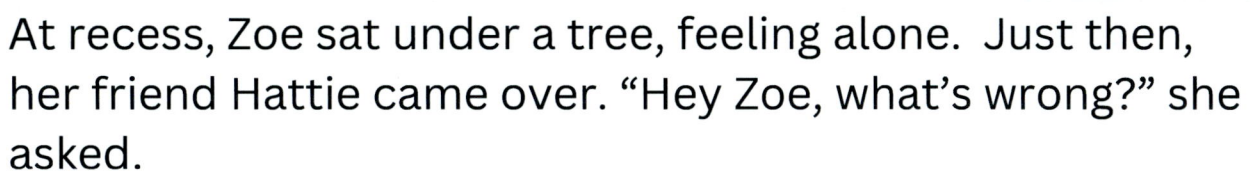

Hattie thought for a moment. "But you are already amazing, Zoe!" You're good at drawing, you make the best stories, and you always have the most creative ideas."

Zoe smiled a little. "I do like making up stories."

Hattie smiled. "Exactly! Maybe your stories don't look like everyone else's, but they are special. You see things in a way that nobody else does. Your mind is like a treasure chest, full of magic!"

Zoe's heart fluttered. "You really think so?"

"I know so," said Hattie.

Zoe said, "My mom said I have something called dyslexia. It's a big word, but it just means that my brain reads and thinks differently. She said it's not wrong; it's just unique. My mom also said that makes me magical!"

Zoe felt a spark of hope. She had never thought of it like that before. That afternoon, Zoe decided to try something new. Instead of focusing on the words she couldn't read, she decided to let her imagination take the lead.

That evening, as Zoe sat at her desk, she closed her eyes and imagined a magical forest. She saw talking animals, glittering stars, and swirling colors. The words in her book became pictures in her mind, and she began to draw them.

She drew a picture of a purple unicorn, a beautiful rainbow, and a gentle flowing river. As she drew, her stories came alive. She filled the pages with images of the adventures she imagined, even though the letters were still tricky to read.

The next day, Zoe shared her drawings with her class. Her teacher, Mrs. Baker, smiled warmly. "Zoe, these are incredible! You've created a whole new world with your drawings. And look—your words are in there, too, in your own special way."

Zoe beamed. "I think my mind is magical."

Mrs. Baker nodded. "It is, Zoe. And with a little practice, you will find your way to reading and writing in your own time. But never forget that your mind is full of creativity and wonder, and that is something truly special."

As the days went by, Zoe continued to draw and tell her stories. She worked so hard. With the support of her family, teachers, and friends, she started to see the magic in her own learning journey. Her dyslexia wasn't something to be ashamed of - it was a part of what made Zoe, Zoe.

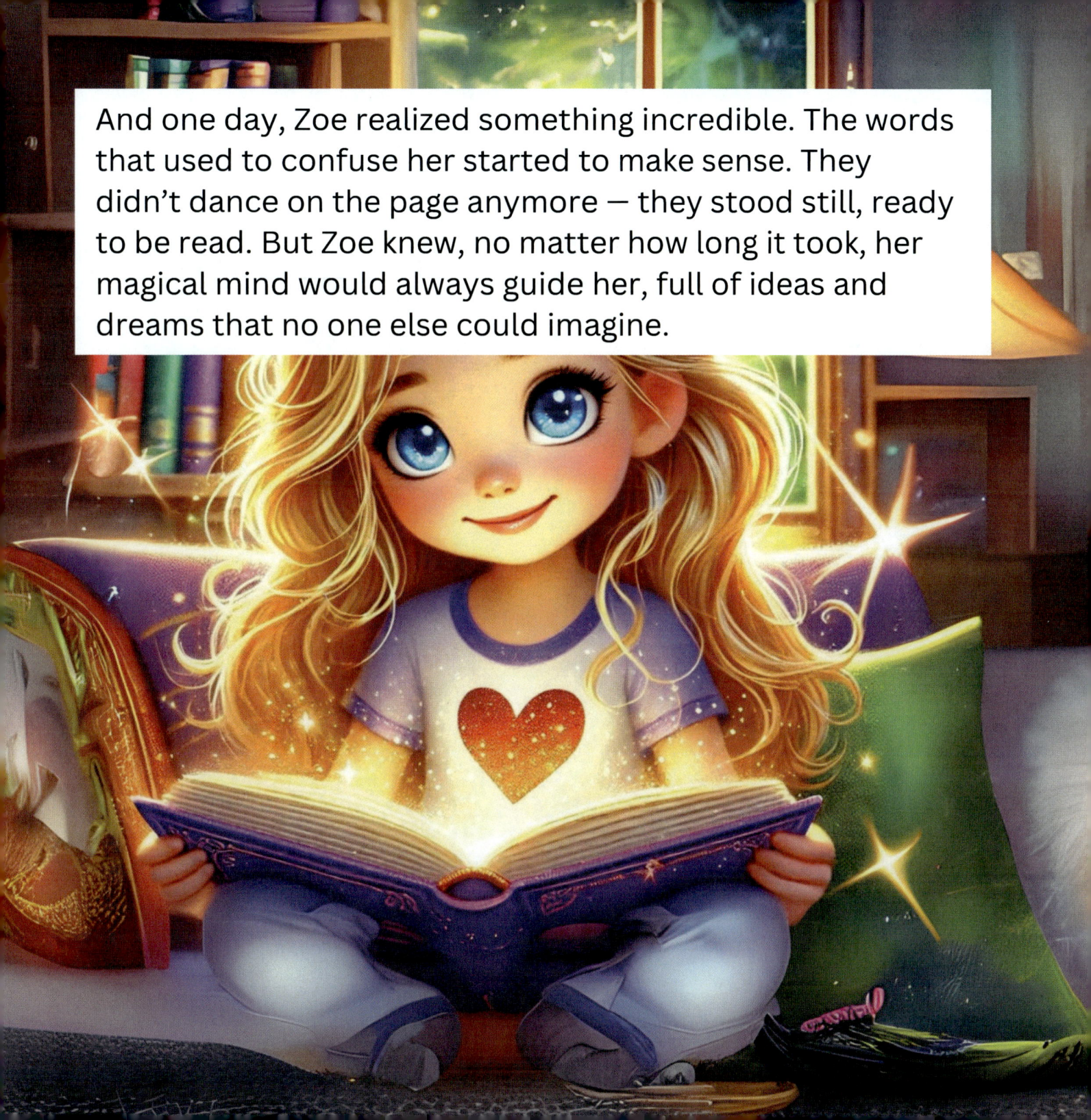

And one day, Zoe realized something incredible. The words that used to confuse her started to make sense. They didn't dance on the page anymore — they stood still, ready to be read. But Zoe knew, no matter how long it took, her magical mind would always guide her, full of ideas and dreams that no one else could imagine.

Zoe smiled, proud of herself, and whispered to the stars outside her window, "Thank you for the magic."

And so, Zoe learned that her mind was not just different—it was wonderfully, beautifully, magical.

Discussion Guide for Parents & Teachers
Zoe's Magical Mind

📖 Understanding the Story

1. How do you think Zoe felt when she realized reading was harder for her than her friends?
2. Why do you think Zoe's mom called her dyslexia a "superpower"?
3. What did Zoe do when she struggled with reading? How did she find a different way to tell stories?
4. How did Zoe's friend Hattie help her feel better?
5. What did Zoe learn about herself by the end of the story?

💡 Thinking About Challenges & Strengths

1. Have you ever found something difficult that seemed easy for others? How did that make you feel?
2. What is something you are really good at? How did you learn to do it?
3. Can you think of other ways to tell a story besides reading and writing?
4. Zoe's mom says her brain works in a special way. What makes your brain special?
5. What advice would you give to someone who feels different from their friends?

♥ Tips for Parents & Teachers:

1. Encourage children to share their thoughts without worrying about "right" or "wrong" answers.
2. Relate Zoe's experience to their own challenges and strengths.
3. Use the creative activities to help children express themselves in different ways.

🎨 Creative Activities 🎨

1. If you could have a magical mind like Zoe, what would it do? Draw or describe your magical mind!

2. Zoe turns words into pictures in her head. Try drawing a scene from your favorite story instead of writing about it.

3. Make a list of words that describe Zoe's superpowers (e.g., creative, smart, brave). What words describe your own strengths?

4. Imagine you are writing a letter to Zoe. What would you tell her about her story?

5. If you could give Zoe a new adventure, what would it be? Make up a short story about her next magical discovery!

Thank you for exploring Zoe's Magical Mind!
This book is designed to inspire children to embrace their unique abilities and find their own magic!

Draw your creative ideas here

Draw your creative ideas here

Draw your creative ideas here

Zoe's Magical Mind is a heartwarming and inspiring story written by Zoe Frank, with love and guidance from her mom, Jennifer Frank. Together, they brought this story to life.

Zoe wanted the world to better understand dyslexia—not as a struggle, but as a unique way of seeing and thinking. She wanted others to experience the world through her eyes, in all its wonderful complexity. While reading and writing sometimes feel like a puzzle, Zoe discovers that her dyslexia isn't a limitation—it's a superpower!

Through imagination, creativity, and a little bit of magic, Zoe learns to embrace her strengths and find new ways to learn. With the support of her family, friends, and a kind teacher, she realizes that her mind isn't broken—it's brilliant!

Perfect for children, parents, and educators, *Zoe's Magical Mind* encourages young readers to celebrate their differences, embrace their gifts, and believe in the magic within them.

Made in the USA
Middletown, DE
09 April 2025

74015149R00015